CONTENTS

SURVIVING A PSYCH WARD

Stigmatized at22

By Leo W. Monfore

INTRODUCING MY STORY

I am 25 years of age as I write this. I come from a typical lower middle class family in America. Our house was rather old and run-down, and since there were six of us children, our parents never really managed to fully renovate it, but hey, it was a roof over our heads and kept us warm and safe. We had the same minor disagreements here and there like any other family. Nothing out of the ordinary. We took road trips, had family gatherings, celebrated holidays, created inside jokes for only us to understand, and grew up together on a typical street in a small city. All of my siblings and I were fortunate enough to be born in what is in my opinion, the greatest two decades for an American childhood: the 80s and 90s. With me as the youngest being born in 1996. The placement of our births definitely played a part in our mentality, futures, and more importantly, lifestyle, which plays a sizable role in my eventual involuntary hospitalization. Being born in a fortunate era, I cannot really find any real complaints to make about my upbringing. I am well aware there are others who had much rougher conditions than me. My father raised me to be an upstanding citizen with a clean moral conscience, and my mother raised me to love everyone unconditionally, without any prejudice or selfishness. Most would agree that this is me winning the lottery at birth being lucky enough to have two loving parents and several older siblings who all took good care of me throughout my childhood, so there is absolutely no room for me to point any fingers at them for any of my shortcomings, as this is a cruel world. This is in no way bragging, and I am sharing this fact to convey that I do not come from a broken home as many with mental illnesses may. The way society tends to throw certain misunderstood demographics into the trash bin without considering nuanced thought so to speak, compels me to write this book and set the record straight on how misinformed most of the public is concerning mental health.

As unusual as this may seem, I have had the privilege of once being "normal" by societal standards, and also becoming what many of my peers steer clear from, mislabeled now as "psychotic" or "a sociopath" by others. The media throws these terms around, whether intentional or not it creates a stigma for many like myself, who under large bursts of inconceivable stress give into our depression and allow it to take us over in the form of self harm or other destructive behaviors. The reason I believe this is a privilege, is that I am able to see from the lens of both groups of people in this world. I believe this stretches beyond the states in many ways, but sadly I can only write on my own experiences in America. Situations undoubtedly similar to mine must be worldwide. I don't believe race, gender, economic status has any true determining factor on one's own mental struggles, which is why I will leave my ethnicity out of this. It wouldn't matter anyways, since I am multiracial. I am a believer that all humans can relate to struggle in the mind.

This is my story of being involuntarily hospitalized for seven days in a psych ward against my will, and the long lasting life changes that continue to be a result from my experience of being locked in there, stripped of my freedom for the very first time in my life, at the unfortunately young age of 22 years old.

CONTRIBUTING FACTORS TO MY ILLNESS

My very first memories on this planet had to be around the age of 3. I was surrounded by loving siblings and parents. Eating cereal on a saturday morning while watching my favorite cartoon on TV, being carried into the kitchen by my elder sister to get a snack, my mother struggling with my stubborn attitude while telling me "It's winter now. You gotta start wearing socks now buddy.", The memories are deeply rooted in my mind. I am also fortunate enough to have a very sharp memory, which will soon be expanded upon too. These were the early years, me just trying to find my place in this brand new family I came into at birth, all of these siblings who predate me. They have been here, having thanksgiving and experiencing life oblivious of my eventual existence. As a young child, everyone in my family would beg me to say some words. I was a mute since birth, taking everything in and giving no input.It is said that I rarely ever cried as a baby. My eyes were always looking around, but I never elaborated on any emotion or expression. I was a true thinker. Throughout the formative years, I was often told to speak more, criticized for not participating enough in school. This "weakness" of mine even negatively affected some class grades down the line. I have never been the life of the party so to speak.

One memory of mine from my early years was being separated from my parents for the first time: Being dropped off at preschool.

To any child that age, this is an alien concept for them. Still to this day, I have no idea why I took it so badly back then, more distress than the other little kids in my preschool. I remember begging my mom and dad to take me back home with them, and when I saw them leave me there, I silently panicked. I never wanted to be seen crying, so I choked up and tried to contain my tears and worry, and I approached a little hat rack that was there for playtime, and I said "Hi. wanna be friends?". Looking back, I know this was me attempting to use humor as a way to cope with the feeling I had that my parents were never coming back, similar to how a puppy acts as their owner leaves the driveway for work. This couldn't have alerted anyone that I would be different from others since it is rather common for kids to behave that way on their first day of preschool. The formation of my behavior however, began right there; It was obvious that I was a lone wolf from day one. My daily schedule in preschool consisted of a few minutes of playtime, then our teacher would call us over to sit in a circle to hear her read a book to us while her aid cooked breakfast for us. We washed our hands, then sat at a long table all together, where we were taught manners, how to treat one another."[insert name], may I please have the juice? Thank you". It was required to speak like this. I truly regret my lack of appreciation for this system I was enrolled into at 4 years old. Looking back, I should have realized this program was intended to set us all up for the inevitability of encountering new people throughout our lives, and how to use basic social skills. I definitely missed the mark in this field. There was a little staircase that led up to a second level in that classroom. I never got to see it, because I turned down dozens of offers from teachers and even other students to go up those stairs and explore during playtime because many other kids went up there after our daily breakfast for a final playtime. I always escaped into a corner to play with something, anything that another kid wasn't playing with, just so I could be alone, where my true self was able to come out in its entirety. I always choose to play with the dollhouse, as I have always had a fascination with house building and architecture in general. I thought of it as a girly activity and became slightly embarrassed if I was seen anywhere near that, but looking busy whilst avoiding others has always been my go-to solution to maintain my comfort zone. That damn comfort zone would become my savior and my enemy...

After playtime on warm days, we would sing a cleanup song while putting everything back where we got it, and then run off to the playground outside to play more and wait for our parents or guardians to come pick us up. It seems like a normal pre-k experience.

Honestly, I do not know if this led up to being a determining mental blow or not, but there was one day in late fall that school year when I suffered a significant smack to the head. I was running around the playground before being picked up by my mother, and another kid in the class was also running up the same part of the playground. We collided, and my four year old head slammed into a hard plastic roof typically seen on a kid's playground. I don't remember much after that, besides the fact that the right side of my forehead bruised and left me a bit confused at the moment, disoriented is a better word. I held the one side of my head and wouldn't cry, because I felt doing that would cause the headache to grow worse. I never told anyone what happened because I didn't understand the importance of concussions and head injuries. Still to this day, I wonder if my brain changed that day from the trauma.

On my final day there, my true personality came out. As my mom was walking me out to say goodbye to my teacher for the last time, after all those months of being silent, keeping my head down and backing into a corner, I uttered a phrase saying "see you later freak!" as a sarcastic joke and everyone laughed at the ironic nature of me finally saying something. I finally became energized, knowing I wouldn't have to return there. It seemed being surrounded by strangers drained my socal energy, and separating from them brought the inner life out of me and lifted my mood as a whole. If my mom would have told me I would have to return there the next day, I wouldn't have said anything funny, sarcastic or anything that gives a single soul a glimpse of a personality I possessed. I was only able to express myself when I had the knowledge that I was free from human interaction again. Kindergarten through 5th grade was a tossup for me. I had some pleasant times, and some dark, miserable and shockingly sobering experiences. I believe my generation grew up mentally a little quicker than others before and after us, based on the age we were when 9/11 changed the world. I was 5 and a half years old that day, an elder of my classmates by several months. We were all too little to understand what was actually happening. I was doing what I did best: looking down and paying attention to my own little world, so I wasn't too actively present in everyone else's conversations. The morning announcements were a little different that morning. Our teacher was paying close attention to that little box TV that rolled out on a cart. Everyone has a story about where they were and what they were doing when they first heard the towers were hit. I was just a little kid and had blocked it out of my mind, since I was too young to understand the idea of any of this. At that age, all of my grandparents were alive and well. I had no idea what death even was. The lighthearted cartoons I saw every day never brought this subject up. My parents obviously never told me that everybody dies, so hearing about this was pretty confusing. I have memories of the teachers explaining to us what a skyscraper was. The terms skyscraper and plane immediately appear side by side in my mind to this day, stemming all the way back to that day I learned of both subjects at once. I once asked my mom "aren't skyscrapers those planes in the sky that make the lines like clouds?" heavily due to the correlation between planes and the twin towers taught to me so quickly at an impressionable age, and partly because I thought the term skyscraper was literal. One of the teachers turned on the computers in the back of our classroom and I have a memory of one of my classmates being shown a photo of the world trade center on a computer and being told about where and what it is. While i dont remember the exact conversation in full, I am sure this was the teachers basically educating us early on about the importance of what was taking place that day, that the world isn't going to be all safe and happy, without overtly telling us "oh yeah, this stuff happens. People die". We were only 5, but given the seriousness and history being made right in front of our innocent eyes, It's strange to think this was the very first exposure to the idea of death for most of us. Not our grandparents passing away, not a relative or family friend on their deathbed saying goodbye as previous generations and future generations first learn of it, none of that. It was thousands of people all at once, in a horrible, horrible gruesome way in our homeland. All working men and women who looked like our parents, young and old, gone, just like that. What a shocking lesson to learn at such a young age, when I was supposed to be worrying about how to tie my shoes and spell my name.

The mental seed was still being planted in me in kindergarten from separate situations. My closed in personality and reluctance to social interaction put a huge target on my forehead from the start in the eyes of my extroverted elders. My kindergarten teacher lost patience with me often. I had bowel issues which caused frequent accidents. I visited the nurse's office literally daily. Everyone would stare at me while the teacher sent me out to get embarrassed yet again. After a new pair of pants and my face turning red, I'd get sent home more often than not. I was considered the different kid in my class. Everybody knew it. My parents tried the best they could. This was more of a behavioral issue than a physical health condition. They tried getting me to fix my diet, brought me to doctors to fix this issue, and eventually this frequent accident problem faded away on its own. It appeared that while I knew of dark and horrible realities of life very early on such as death and destruction that dominated the news that year, It seemed to have slowed down my personal maturity development.

Eventually, I made it out of the torturous school year of me being the class fool, and moved on through elementary school as the awkward kid, sort of out of place. I always had one best friend, who fared much better than me socially, having many friends besides me. I had no other friends beyond him, even up until high school. I began noticing a trend each year, every new grade. I just wasn't understanding anything. Academically I technically was passing everything. It was grade school, so being the next Einstein wasn't really required of me. The aspect I couldn't grasp was how personal everything had to be. In the logical sense, the purpose of school is to learn the basic structure of what society is and what to expect. I just felt gym class was a waste of time, meant to open opportunities of bullying, and embarrass students who were not athletic. Assigned seats also made no sense to me, an arbitrary rule designed without consideration of the personal needs of certain individuals with anxiety or those who simply get work done in a certain spot much better. I lost focus on lessons so often thanks to having a front seat forced on me while everyone behind me stared and joked about how I was the kid a couple years back in kindergarten who always had accidents and things like that. All in all, my opinion on the lack of empathy some educators show to slower and unpopular students in many cases hasn't changed.

Middle school was very rough compared to elementary, to the point of several anxiety attacks, beginning my downward spiral into a mental health dilemma for me. I was thrusted into this brand new world, with three times the amount of students than I had been previously used to seeing. Due to the placement of this junior high school being centralized, There were kids from wealthy households from the other side of town who wore much different clothing than I was accustomed to. They spoke differently than my peers from the lower middle class area I came from. They were the first ones my age I witnessed having girlfriends and boyfriends for the first time, and these students excelled in sports as well as clubs pretty often. The concept of popularity, physical appearance, status and perception began emerging as a constant metaphorical trophy at this age. For the first time, not only was I no longer the only awkward kid in school, but I was also now on the bottom of some pyramid scheme, a rating system split up into categories and a tower to climb. Your best was never good enough in this place. In my grade school, I grew familiarity of everyone and at least they knew who I was and what to expect of me, but here in this foreign world with fresh faces, I was hammered with the reality that I needed to start all over again from scratch with new people and try presenting myself as mainly a normal kid in this first impression i had to give to everyone in those hallways. With all of the cliques and different personalities minding their own business for the most part, I remained rather under the radar for the early stages of middle school. However, this was a violent school. Every day there was a rumor floating around of some kid planning a fight outside at lunch time or after school, sometimes in the gym. It was constant. Mixing a diverse group of people from varying backgrounds and wealth can prove to be both fruitful. And evidently problematic, and my school was a perfect example of this. I was caught up in the random violence that occurred during recess. I cannot count the amount of times I was chased down and knocked silly onto the blacktop. There was one bully in particular, who looked down on me. I never really got to find out why, but he simply enjoyed using me as his punching bag. For every 5 day week, 2 or 3 of those days he would approach me. Sometimes it was a simple insult, a gentle push against a fence telling me to move, or a slap in the face, and then there were the brutal beatings. I had days where he'd slam me down to the concrete, kick me, stomp my head in, etc. I was certainly not the only student dealing with this kind of bullying. I witnessed others suffer much worse fates than my own. A few times I would see fights become very serious in a heartbeat. One kid a grade above me once had his arm completely broken in a fight after school. The point mainly being made is that this school was generally not very welcoming for most young men who were not cliqued up or protected by a flock of their own. Grades 6 through 8 tested my mental limits without mercy. I never ended up finding my place in that crowd. Adrift in an uncaring cluster of personalities, I faded more and more into obscurity, while my best friend from earlier years became more popular by the day. An introspective person such as myself reflects on our own insecurities by watching a best friend outpace us as we stay at the bottom socially. The same person who was on the same page as me on the playground, shaped up to be a totally different energy than me to others.

By the time highschool approached, I was already tired of everything. I quit the world for a few years after ninth grade. I became a highschool dropout after only a year of attending. Sometimes I ask myself why I made such a dangerous choice like this, but I remembered what kind of environment I was experiencing. One moment in ninth grade caused quite a bit of trauma for me, and it involved internet tactics kids used back then to humiliate others to make themselves laugh. Someone who was pretending to be my friend, unbeknownst to me, would go on social media and publicly ridicule me, and come up with false detrimental rumors, smearing my name for everyone to see. This crippled any chances of me having an honest chance befriending anyone in his circle, or anyone in my grade for that matter. Those days were the beginning of everyone having a social media account. Naturally, the vast majority of our peers in our age group were mutual friends through somebody and frequented these internet spaces to face off in this popularity contest through their profiles. Most classmates heard damaging false rumors about me, spread by students who hated my eccentric personality so much, to the point of creating fake profiles online pretending to be me, and creating additional fake profiles of others pretending to befriend me as well. The rumors were created as a joke by bored adolescents to find entertainment in the weirdest person they could think of, and I was the target. They had no idea how damaging this type of bullying could be to my mental perception of people. There were times I would go home and stuff my face with any food in my kitchen to ease the stress I felt from having to show my face in a sea of magnifying glasses all looking at me. I was becoming popular for all the wrong reasons. The day I walked down the hallway and overheard a group of kids I hung around with snickering while reading quotes from that social media page referencing jokes about me, with no provocation from me whatsoever, sealed my decision to give up on trying to become a sociable guy.I believe I would have had a chance to become something that is now out of my reach. High School in the movies always typically portrayed young men and women going out with friends, learning how to drive for the first time, making a lot of friends and taking a million photos at prom, planning out college and thinking of possible career ideas, etc. None of this was true to me. My experience in highschool was a nightmare, and ended before it had a chance to begin. Life at home was completely normal throughout school before dropping out, with nothing out of the ordinary. The only atypical thing was always me throwing my homework to the side. It's not like my parents didn't encourage me to do the work. They became mad when I refused to do my assignments like many parents do. As my mid teens went on, I disconnected from everyone. No social media presence, not a single friend, no goals or ambitions. I could not foresee the next year, let alone ten years after.

After two years of being stagnant, my parents finally convinced me to think about the future, and I attempted to obtain my high school equivalency diploma from a poorly funded school in a rough neighborhood. Since I was still a minor and had not completed 10th grade, I had to attend classes before taking on that exam. I cannot establish if I was the blame, or if my instructor was to blame. We simply got off on the wrong foot almost immediately at first sight. In a way, he was the anti-me. I really couldn't concentrate unless I was left alone and given the choice to remain in the background, and he insisted on making me the center of attention every session. I greatly took offense to this, as I warned him before signing up, that I for whatever reason cannot do much social interaction and needed to just hear the lesson and learn from it in the form of my work. He knew from my parents also telling him that I had more social anxiety than a typical 16 year old, and that I could do the work just fine if I was left alone without any unnecessary conversation. This guy still yelled for no reason, almost blaming me as a human on a personal level for not understanding the way he worded a certain math question for example. My sensitivity to criticism at the time didn't help matters, coming from an entire childhood of being pointed at and put down by my peers, I finally snapped one day in class. The teacher in this GED class went through the average routine of passing out papers and mentioned the previous day when I was especially quiet largely due to a random bout of depression. There are times a feeling of impending doom washes over my entire mind, as if everything is wrong and something terrible is coming my way. These random overwhelming feelings of pure dread come and go randomly, with no cause most of the time. I zoned out the day before, and he brought it up afterwards asking what was wrong with me. The word "wrong" bothered me, with the tone of voice being used and the generally judgemental feeling i got from him. I essentially freaked out for the first time on anyone. I had piled up stress and anxiety about my future bottling up, preventing me from thinking straight, so I had a regretful knee jerk reaction to him, which was lashing out in a full blown argument. For the first time, the mute kid who had his head down all the time began biting back. Curse words were used, I was expressing my annoyance with my teacher as if he personally wronged me, all based on one insensitive comment he made to me. I began to realize what my anxiety is truly capable of turning me into. I don't like the way I was that day, and I never wanted to act that way again. Fate however, contradicted what I wanted, versus what was ultimately bound to happen again in the coming years. I grew more and more impatient with people, more brash, a little more attitude. I began reflecting dirty looks back at people in the form of the middle finger and an insult.

My late teens were a transformative time for me, possibly one of the greatest eras of my life. I got my first job at a factory in town, prompting me to become busy and occupied really for the first time. I was living an adult life and enjoying it. The social pyramid of adolescence became distant in my rear view mirror as I became the greatest version of myself. Nothing special happened in these few years. From 18 to 22 I blended right into society without issue, at least I thought I did. Even at my job (which I stayed at for 4 years) I still was known by everyone as the quiet guy. Coworkers would often make ignorant jokes about my demeanor, saying things like "that guy looks like he's gonna kill everyone". These inflammatory statements offended me as someone who prided myself on having a squeaky clean record with the law. I have always kept to my own business and treated others with respect. Sure all of my interactions with others remained awkward at best, but I tried managing the best I could in a large company with so many strangers, and showed unconditional friendliness with everyone. I will always pat myself on the back for this accomplishment. I eventually became a good worker, and earned the respect of my supervisors enough to be considered worth keeping. Nobody knew that I was hiding a dark secret trapped in my mind. Beneath my calm and mild mannered personality everyone there knew me as, at home I would cut myself where no one would be able to see it. This facade was good enough to hide until the stress release required more bold scars to fill the void, but what *was* my void in the first place? As I type this, I wholeheartedly have no idea. This is the scariest aspect of the reasoning behind my behavior. I do know however, that while I never figured out what I am missing in life, I cannot deny why cutting was the eventual channel for me to take out my stress, albeit unhealthy.

This will later be explained, but a main focal point of my writing here is to convey a new perspective. While medical professionals are bright and know the human body and brain, the human personality and mind is not necessarily proven to be created by the brain, rather it seems to take a seat in the brain while in the body. A person's true intentions are not determined by brain chemicals. Yes they influence and play a large factor, but my brain isn't me. I have that brain, it does not have me. The automatic go-to phrase a medical professional will tell someone when they cut themselves is the classic "You do not love yourself if you harm yourself". This is plainly not true for all who suffer with mental illness, and I will describe this theory's flaws in a later chapter. This sentence was told to me several times in the years to come. This is a blanket statement that doesn't serve as a sincere way to figure out a person's illness.

Back to the events leading up to my emergency admission. In 2017, life had been going pretty well for me. I had a healthy relationship with everybody. I was close to my parents, siblings, girlfriend, and had a job paying me enough to take care of a home I rented, and kept my car fueled up each week to go about my life. I even took the occasional road trip on weekends. I had everything I really needed. My awkwardness remained, and people still often gawked at me looking stiff and awkward each time I went grocery shopping, but generally, I felt okay with myself regardless of how weird I looked to others. Somehow I still felt though, that I wasn't truly experiencing a completely full life. I would often see others with more money than me, pretending to appear to be happier than others, with newer cars and didn't rent their homes, but owned them instead. This is where my greed took over and I stupidly convinced myself I needed just a little more. At the time, my job field was considerably low paying, and the hyper social dynamic of that building was taxing on my brain, not to mention having to wake up at 4 AM every day. I began looking for a higher paying job in a different field; What a colossal mistake. That decision of discontent bred several years of a personal hell that I haven't fully recovered from. I got into contact with another employer who had a job lined up for me in maintenance of a garage. It was going to be much higher paying by a factor of a few dollars more than my previous job. It was going to be hard physical work, but limited interaction with people. It sounded perfect for me, so I went for it. I put all of my eggs in that basket, and trusted this manager's words that he would get me into that place, because he had already been an acquaintance of mine from years prior. Before working my first job, I did a short month of cleaning around that workplace for him. My naive 21 year old mind trusted his words alone, so I began preparing to start working for him in the coming month. I quit my job of 3 and 1/2 years at that point, as the early mornings and human interaction completely wore me out by then, and believed I had enough money to hang on until I got that call back from him saying he's ready for me to start work. Days passed and I wasn't panicking whatsoever. I kept telling my girlfriend everything was fine and I would be working there in a couple weeks and we'd be moving into a nicer house with more space. Those two weeks passed and now I started worrying. I attempted calling that manager back several times, and no pickup. He was a busy man, dealing with hundreds of people a day. It would be easy to forget that he mentioned I can come work for him again. The hiring process for my job title there was fairly casual. All it required was for me to come in, fill out a paper, then I'm off to cleaning floors and bathrooms, just as it would have been the first time I worked for him. I honestly believed it would be a quick process. I continued to call every few days hoping to get into contact with the manager, and nothing ever came of it. I couldn't go back to the other job I just quit. Panic started setting into place, causing me to think of ways to hold off and save money to pay for my house until he called back. I sold items around my home I rarely used in the beginning of this period. First it was my bicycle, then my old video game systems, my guitars, some books, then after a month and a half, I knew he changed his mind about hiring me. Other things came up. I wasn't going to be landing that job. Back then, I believed everyone was out to get me, but now I know this was my fault anyways. Since I was little, I had a bad habit of mishearing people, having a lack of social skills, and misunderstood people's words and took them as gospel truth most of the time. I was the kid who heard the word grocery store and believed that guaranteed I would be leaving there with candy, meaning I was easy to disappoint. I was out of my mind and emanated true foolishness hearing the words "we need a cleaner. We want you back here!", and translating it to "You are first in line for a job. You will be starting next month". Why did I quit my job before being guaranteed anything? Why couldn't I just have waited to see what happened before burning bridges? Pure delusion more than anything! I mistook someone's words, and I paid a brutal price for it.

As the months went on, my finances dwindled. After selling every personal item of any worth, then went my new couches, watches I owned, then finally, my house. I was in no position to keep renting that place, and I knew finding a brand new job was going to be grueling. It was already hard enough for me, after being a highschool dropout with zero social experience whatsoever and a very limited skillset, to settle into my first real job and become halfway comfortable there. Willingly showing up to a business with 200 people all approaching me so early in the morning with their unsolicited smiles and small talk, for such little pay was a true credit to my determination to create a better life for myself, and though mentally straining to have to go through each day, this task has been supplying the good life I had outside of work. I owed everything to that annoying job I thought of as such a hardship. Moving back in with my parents was surely not my first choice, but was seen as necessary. Without this option I would have been living under a bridge somewhere begging for food. I hadn't slept in that house since 2015 before I moved out for the first time at the age of 19. I took for granted the personal freedom of living independently, as I was being completely pulled into other people's organization habits, time management and schedules, bedtimes, diets, and everything else that comes along with lifestyle. I truly forgot how much I absolutely hated hearing about my parent's coworkers and topics they find interesting that I have no part of. I was a simple guy; I enjoyed watching baseball, writing in a journal, taking walks in my neighborhood, playing musical instruments, and sitting on my porch back home, NOT being confined to one room, having my items misplaced by others, being forced to place three bedrooms worth of furniture into one small bedroom, etc. This was a totally different atmosphere. My parents are now middle aged. The home I once grew up in, was now a relic with spare rooms filled with junk where my siblings and I once stayed. My energy was that of a guy who loved my peace and quiet. I didn't belong sharing space with others, especially after I've tasted the freedom of being my own man in my own house. There was clearly room for me to live there, but it definitely didn't sit right with me. I had to share a tiny bathroom the size of a chicken coop, with 2 other people. The cupboards in there were all theirs, as was the fridge in the kitchen and the arrangement of the living room. The driveway was theirs, the porch was theirs. Though they offered for me to arrange in any way I needed for personal space and comfort, It just didn't work. I left my parents at the age of 19. I had barely become an adult and learned to separate my personal life from theirs. I became used to it. Two years seems like nothing, but my time spent on my own was more than enough to establish the fact that I knew I needed my own place, and It worked perfectly for me. The depression of being back to square one spiraled me into fits of rage. Not outwardly, but bottling day by day. My girlfriend and I started arguing more often than usual over little things that hardly ever mattered and I began noticing patterns in my own behavior that were running rampant. Her family and friends began hating me, doubting me and told her that I wasn't good enough to be with her and that I was a low level loser. This hurt my self esteem to the point where I would have bouts of depression. I have applied for several other jobs since then, all of which gave me an opportunity. So what is the problem?

Each time I mustered the courage to try something new, I would get the call from the employer, and would ask me to attend an interview. Things looked good. For half of the jobs, I actually went in for the interviews. My awkward personality and terrible lack of eye contact and general issues still persisted, but I nonetheless got these jobs. From November 2017, to July 2018, I had job offers from dozens of employers, and worked at 2 more factory jobs, for only one week each before quitting without notice. The pattern was taking shape at this point. I knew that each time I got a call about a job, that I wouldn't actually see it through to the end. I somehow knew nothing would work out, yet I kept applying for any and every job I could find online, fully aware that I mentally wouldn't fare too well in any of these environments. I had a specific guideline I gave myself to follow pertaining to what will and will not be a career choice that would lead up to more panic attacks and quitting within the first month and still, I applied halfheartedly to several different avenues in all directions, in desperation to get out of this terrible situation. My checking account constantly had around 3 dollars sitting in it. I would often overdraft to keep my vehicle fueled enough to still be able to go see my girlfriend , who I was terrified would decide to leave me at any moment if I didn't get my act right. I might as well have closed my savings account considering it has been empty for months. I ran out of resources. I had forgotten all songs I could previously play from start to finish, from the lack of personal space that I definitely need to be able to focus. The neighborhood became more run down than it has ever been. Known criminals began moving in and out of our street each month, with their own set of drama plaguing the block in intervals, so taking my neighborhood walks was out of the question. I could no longer find a good time to read or write in my journal, thanks to the fact that now I am living on my parent's schedules. Bedtime was 3 AM. It takes me a few hours to fully settle in to be able to fall asleep, and my parents going to sleep at 11 PM most nights made it very difficult for me to have any time to take care of my personal hygiene before they slept, so I would often begin brushing my teeth and take my showers as late as midnight some nights, because I knew I wouldn't be awake early enough the next day to get ready while they work, because I had an obligation to fulfill. I may have messed up my partner's peace, but I was still her boyfriend, and I wasn't going to let any of this serve as an excuse to not continue seeing her, as I believe while finances and a bottom of the barrel situation can harm a relationship, It still does not take anything away from a bond one has with another human. This is still earth and we are people.

WIth midnight onwards being the only time of complete silence and alone time I could have, that was the main time I would work in my journals, read books and listen to music in my headphones as a routine to get myself tired enough to be able to get some sleep. I had no time to even consider practicing my passion playing several instruments, so my talent progressively got worse and worse, until I could no longer call it a talent anymore. This new schedule change metaphorically killed me. I was completely drained from overeating, laying around with no job, and falling asleep at the same time I would have been waking up had I kept that job I pretended to hate so much. Everything was backwards in the worst way. In my previous lifestyle, I had a very clean and modest diet and a workout routine. Everything in my home was as organized as a doctor's office. Clean and simple was my motto. I went from that, to now being thrusted into eating someone else's diet, while having nothing but time stuck in this house eating snacks to both kill the boredom and to relieve my stress and not having the money to go buy my own balanced meals. I couldn't really complain as I was still being fed, but my health began declining shortly thereafter.

POLICE DETAINMENT, EMERGENCY HOSPITALIZATION

It was a hot summer day towards the end of July in 2018. I argued daily up to that point with both my girlfriend as well as my parents. These arguments intertwined since we unfortunately all shared space in one house leading up to it. That thursday evening I visibly had been frustrated and angry from an argument I had earlier with my partner about personal quarrels we were having with our peers, plus a situation we got ourselves into walking around an art store where a guy was staring at me and ridiculing me with his eyes based on my uncomfortable mannerisms while walking around a public place and the pressure of needing to look for another job building up prior to it, and my parents naturally overheard me crying angrily and throwing my phone against the wall, smashing it entirely in a full blown anxiety attack. My father attempted calming me down but it only ended in another argument with him because I was too pent up to lower my own voice. In a burst of rage, I flipped a table over with papers all over the place and stormed out of the house with both parents attempting to stop me. I was completely in a trance and was turned off from the world. All I could think of in my mind at the time was "Get out of the house. Go somewhere that is clear of any humans to catch your breath, otherwise you will never relax", so i drove for nearly 2 hours (without a phone or contact with anyone), rightfully worrying everyone in my family and my girlfriend who hasn't witnessed me that tense before, even if it was just an argument over the phone. This was the first time my parents have ever witnessed me scream at the top of my lungs as well. Completely unaware of it, my parents went out to get me another cheap prepaid phone to use while I was out driving. After the meltdown I had in their house, They were still thoughtful enough to buy me something I really didn't deserve in the first place and it was all my fault. By the time I got back home, the house was silent. Nobody said a word to each other besides the usual goodnight. I had thought everything died down and I let my anger fully out, which is partially true in the physical sense. By this time, my parents found out about my cutting. I was hiding from everyone for a few years and this caused panic. My dad mentioned a program where the police come for a welfare check on someone who is thought to be a danger to themselves or others for mental reasons and are taken away to the mental hospital never to be seen again. I sincerely didn't believe at the time the police had that kind of power to chime into my personal life like that, so I blew it off and went on with the rest of my weekend. From thursday onwards, my girlfriend would not let me see her in fear that I would lash out at her the same way I did with my parents and didn't want my drama. I can't blame her. Afterall I was causing much more trouble than it was worth. This bothered me though, since the mounting stress and anger in me caused by a vast multitude of problems such as being poor and lost my entire lifestyle, along with the way people treated me when I dared go into public trying to fit in, all combined with relationship problems was proving to be too much for my brain to handle. All I needed those few days was to relax, and to know everything will be okay, and when my girlfriend spent the whole friday and weekend ignoring my texts I definitely didn't feel as though things were going to be okay ever again. I was fully convinced I had lost her for good. By the time Monday came around, I grew frustrated and began pleading to at the very least be notified if she left me for good, or if she was just ignoring me and needed space. The mixed signals were adding to the flames to me. She agreed to see me that day and while taking a walk at a park, she noticed my tense behavior once again. Our day was cut short because of her fear for her own safety. Again, looking back it is all perfectly reasonable for her to give up on me. A human cannot carry an entire person's hardships on top of their own by themselves. She had a life and a college degree she was busy obtaining. My sudden change in character and anger became too large of a threat to her own future success. It would have been incredibly difficult to live with that kind of fear and uncertainty while trying to study hard in college at the same time.

The next day approached, the day that would change the course of my entire future goals and lifestyle. Tuesday began normal enough for what it was. Another day without a job in the old run-down home. The arguing in text form was subtle but still there. I hadn't officially broken up with at that point, but she had basically given up on me and wanted to just study, which should be the priority of anyone in college. I still to this day am still foreign to anything academia related from my early exodus from the school system, so I lacked understanding of her need to study or do anything education wise for that matter. I kept pushing and pushing for more insight on why I was being ignored rather than being reasoned with. The messages coming from me then shifted to cursing, pretending I didn't care, then I tried ignoring her back in an attempt to see if she would cave and ask if i'm okay. The lengths I went for one person, while fully knowing what the outcome would be was not healthy in the slightest, especially since it was by my own actions responsible for pushing her away. My text messages grew more desperate, grabbing for attention mostly. I would try every manipulative measure in the book to receive a reaction to know she was still paying attention.

The decision that changed it all approached. I began sending dangerous threats as a scare tactic. The threats included bodily harm to myself and to others. One of the sentences I typed included a phrase "Okay! Won't listen? Okay *i'll just kill everyone then lol*! Okay! Bye!" or something to that effect. While I cannot recall the text verbatim, it did include threats to actually kill others, even though I had absolutely no intentions whatsoever to even hurt a fly. The reasoning behind my harmful text messages was a means to grab attention. It was a ploy for her reaction, to end the silence. Saying such a false yet damning threat was the final straw for everyone. My girlfriend eventually forwarded those aggressive text messages to my relatives without my knowledge, and that is where everything changed in an instant. At the time while sending the threatening messages, I had headphones on in my bedroom full blast. My plan was to block out everything and everyone until I felt better. I knew myself enough to know being alone with my thoughts was the only remedy to anger and anxiety; It always has been , ever since that dollhouse in the corner in pre-k, but this was different. I was now a fully grown man with a stubble on my face and a credit score, who had just transmitted text messages threatening to go nuts in an instant. The cuteness of me being the shy kid who hated when people looked at me has worn off. This was now a very serious adult matter. Everyone in my family was terrified of me, and my girlfriend most of all. By the time 3:30 PM came around, I was laying in my bed listening to music finally fully relaxed. I assumed that once I sent those intimidating threatening messages, she would see it and eventually be forced to respond to me, so I put the phone down for a while to decompress. While the music blared in my ears, I could hear a knock on my door and a man saying "Hey Leo?" Since my sense of hearing was slightly restricted due to the loud music, I thought maybe my brother in law had come by to visit me to hang out as he did from time to time, so I took the headphones off and yelled "What up?" as a typical greeting I usually used with him. Again a knock, and this time my ears were freed and I heard a total authoritative voice I was unfamiliar with sternly explaining in a gruff voice, calmly but with volume "LEO, WE ARE WITH THE SHERIFF'S DEPARTMENT. WE GOT A CALL THAT YOU WERE THREATENING BODILY HARM. OPEN UP."

My stomach completely dropped. I was utterly shocked. I had no idea how to process this. I had never had any interactions with police beforehand besides one speeding ticket. They must have heard me get up out of bed because they continued on "DO YOU HAVE ANY WEAPONS OR ANYTHING THAT WOULD HARM US IN ANY WAY.". I write this in the form of a sentence, and not a question. I could tell this officer has done this type of call alot. His lines seemed rehearsed in a way, as if it was a day to day scenario grown accustomed to. I told them that no I didn't have any weapons and that I was opening the door and we will talk. But I did annoyingly say "Come on. She called the cops on me now?!" This was immediately when I opened up that door. The first officer in my sight was in my kitchen, hand on his waistband just in case, because there is no way to know what would happen in that situation from their perspective. This police officer looked to be only a couple years older than me. He could have been my sibling. He was that young. I poked my head out into the hallway and a big and tall, very intimidating officer of an older age towered over me. He was the most frightening presence in that house. This officer served as the brick wall between me and a door or escape route. The younger cop was the one leading the conversation with me. I believe this was likely an intentional method to use an officer in their twenties who would be able to relate more with me. Admittedly it did help quite a bit, since if it was the large older officer in my hallway doing the talking, I would have likely been much more terrified to speak.

I went on to describe my part of the story "I'm not gonna do anything. I shouldn't have said any of that. What? You never uttered the phrase that you'll kill so and so in a sarcastic way?" He pushed back in defiance of my lame excuse. The conversation lacked understanding, yet I could tell there was empathy coming from him. I believe this college aged officer imagined himself being in that situation himself, had he gone down a similar path as mine. This was a man to man conversation, plain and simple.

After glancing down the hallway, I noticed my sister, who did not live with me, was in the living room witnessing the entire thing unfold. I remember being more embarrassed than anything. I thought to myself "Great. Now everyone knows about my personal life. She is going to tell her kids about this and they will never look up to me again. I probably just lost my entire family." I told the officer I won't continue talking to him until she goes outside to the porch because I didn't want her seeing me in that condition. She went outside and the police notified me that legally, they were required to bring me to the hospital for evaluation. Assuming this would be a quick little scolding from a doctor then I'd be sent off with meds, I reluctantly agreed to go with the cops. I asked if I had a choice and if I would go to jail if I said no and they were adamant that I would face criminal charges if I refused treatment, based on the severity of threats said in my text messages. The threats were not towards my girlfriend in particular, but to basically everyone that we knew at the time as a whole, mainly as a scare tactic to force her to talk to me. I knew hospitalization would be inevitable in the end game, but the most regretful part was the way I just threw everyone in my life into this mental breakdown by claiming I would harm them if my girlfriend didn't respond to my texts. It was so stupid. I knew it was immediately when I pressed send. There could have been millions of different ways to get her attention besides claiming some unrealistic nonsense that I would have never done, not that there should have been any method in the first place. I should have just put the phone down that week and let her decide whether or not she would fill me in on what our status is on her own time. The selfishness of my actions brought everyone to be fearful. There were no actual harmful intentions or wishes, but even the words being typed in my text messages were enough to be seen as dangerous and they needed to take me away to protect everyone, even including myself, as my texts also entailed cutting myself, which alarmed them enough to see the scars on my arms from previous cutting. They had no way of knowing that I wasn't going to do anything at all and I was basically attempting psychological abuse and fear into my girlfriend's anxious mind

So the officers walked me towards my front door, and I remember saying "Okay, let's head out then." and the younger officer said "Well, we unfortunately have to cuff you. It is the process of a call like this. For our own safety we are required to detain you in this situation. You are not under arrest, but we believe you are mentally ill, and we don't really know what you are capable of because we don't know you, so we need to do this for legal reasons". I respectfully complied, explaining they were just doing their jobs and before exiting that front door, I proclaimed "Alright guys. Let's just get this over with.". As I stepped outside, I saw at least 6 cop cars outside, with maybe 10 officers standing both on my porch, and on the street. Both of my parents were home. I felt so guilty that they actually left work early, all because I had to be dramatic. I remember walking past my parents and my sister and couldn't look them in the eye. As the officers walked me down the stairs I calmly muttered "I don't want to talk to any of you right now. Tell my girlfriend what's happening please." My parents told me later on, that they thought I meant I didn't want to talk to them because I was angry with them, but the truth is that I said I didn't want to talk with them because I was ashamed, and had nothing to say at the time because all i could think about is my girlfriend. That was my first priority at hand. I had no time to discuss anything with my parents. It was nothing personal.

An officer took me to a squad car and let me lean on the hood to rest with the painful steel handcuffs on, while a social worker in body armor approached me with a clipboard. I was petrified and still in a great deal of shock at that moment in time. She introduced herself and asked me a number of personal questions about mental health, and what I think led me to be in that predicament. She was friendly, as her job required. I looked around and could see many of the officers with the expression on their faces as if to say "This was what we got called out here for?" A couple of the officers had their shotguns strapped to their backs, ready for whatever happens. This must have been a pretty serious report. I never got to hear the specifics on what my relatives told the police on the phone, but they viewed my texts from my girlfriend's screenshots, and that was all they needed to see from there. The police obviously also viewed that private conversation. No one pressed charges, since everyone was in consensus I was tackling a detrimental mental health crisis, even several months beforehand. It was shaping and fairly noticeable to anyone who saw me on a daily basis. They felt mental evaluation would be better than jail. My parents told the young officer who previously talked to me that I was never a violent individual in my entire life, and that I have no history of abuse or physical fights. Not once have I laid a finger on anyone around me. It was elaborated further by my mom and dad on the porch, that I was showing signs weeks ago of bottled stress and it appeared to them that I was reaching a breaking point in my life and let the anxiety consume me. The younger officer approached me again when I was done being interviewed by the social worker, and told me that he could tell I wasn't a bad guy, and that he arrests actual violent people all the time, and this was different on the basis that I was experiencing mental illness. The evidence of an illness piled up once the cops were told that these types of ailments ran in the family tree as well. Either way, I was still quite a bit shell shocked from everything that just occurred to me, and could not process what he was actually telling me, and I didn't know the difference between being detained and being arrested, so I still thought I was off to jail regardless.

Two guys with bulletproof vests stepped me up into a van that was used to transport jailhouse inmates. The reality kicked in and my heart started racing, as I uncomfortably sat myself on this cold, metal seat in the back of that van, with the handcuffs on so tight, my hands felt like the circulation was being cut off and that they would have to be amputated. When those doors shut, the back compartment I was seated inside became dark like a tunnel, with my only light being from this miniscule caged window on the back door of the van. Each time the van accelerated and turned, I would start sliding back and forth on the slippery metal of the seats since there wasn't any arm rests or support, forcing me to use my numbing constricted hands as a stabilizer on the wall behind me, only causing the cuffs to dig further into my wrist until my face physically winced from the pain. A thousand thoughts were jumbling together in my mind while on that ride to the hospital. "Am I going to jail? What if they are just lying about the hospital to get me to agree to come? What if I never see anyone again? I really messed up this time. God please kill me. I don't want this life anymore if it will be spent locked up. Please end it. Please. She is already out cheating on me. I just know it. I can't do this". I actually prayed in that seat for God to end my life. That is how hopeless my outlook was on the entire outcome. I truly believed it would be the end of my life as I knew it. That 10 minute ride in handcuffs felt like 2 months to me, given the excruciating pain of the handcuffs cutting my wrists. That was my first and last time being placed in handcuffs in my life, but I don't want to imagine how others feel while detained if they have thicker wrists than mine. The van finally approached the emergency entrance of the local hospital after what seemed like forever, and I was led to step down out of the van. I told the cop those handcuffs were torture devices. The younger officer from before brought me into the emergency room with others following him. Looking back, I think this call was *his* case. He seemed to be the main one dealing with me the most. They were his handcuffs after all. Upon entering the waiting room for the ER, I immediately drew everyone's attention with my large police escort and handcuffs. The officer finally uncuffed me and told me that there were no charges on me and that he urged me to play this safely and not to exacerbate anything so that I get through this process, get the help I need, and stay out of trouble afterwards. This was encouraging to know that at least I wasn't headed to jail or to see a judge, and that all I had to do in theory was deal with these medical people then leave. I was seated in the waiting room with every eye on me there. The social worker approached me again with more papers and explained that she would be in contact with my parents and was overlooking my case from there. I looked up to the clock and it was past 4:30 PM. I couldn't believe only an hour passed from the time I sent those texts until I landed myself in the hospital. The entire process for me felt like an entire day due largely to my conscience being warped from trauma and fear.

The waiting room was the easy part. Soon they brought me into the actual emergency room, where I was told to remove my shoes. Why? I would soon find out. I sat in one of the beds assigned to me, while hearing a person with a possible fractured leg groaning, an elderly drunk man cursing at the staff, then proclaiming his love for them in the same sentence, and a lot of busy employees going about their work. I sat there, waiting and waiting with my phone in hand, not only to be seen by a doctor, but to hear from anyone. My parents did text me with encouragement for what I was going through, as well as some other relatives offering support. I was never alone on this journey luckily, but I surely felt like it. Because I uttered the words "I don't want to talk to any of you right now", my parents took it literally, and did not accompany me in the emergency room. I was stressed out and embarrassed to notice many people I had gone to school with working in this hospital, and I can tell they immediately recognized me. Everything was out in the open at this point. I lost all credibility as a good person in the public eye. A hospital tech brought me a tray of food. It was an unappealing looking bowl of tomato soup, a cookie, and some milk. I refused to touch that tray. My stomach was so upset and my mind and heart raced so fast, that even the smell of any food would cause me to throw up. Waiting around turned into an ordeal for me. I looked at the clock on my phone the whole time I sat in that uncomfortable bed. An entire 4 hours passed before something, *anything* happened. Around 8:45 or so, I looked at the clock on my phone one last time. A doctor finally came around to take my blood and run some additional tests on me. She contacted another worker after my evaluation, and I thought I was finally done. I felt slight relief, knowing the worst was probably over in my foolish mind. I thought she was going to send me off with medicine and I would get back home. This couldn't be farther from the truth. I was approached by this worker, a nurse or a tech, I do not know, but she notified me that I had to give her my phone. She had put it inside of a brown bag, along with all of my other belongings and That would be the last time i see it for now. She began walking me down a hallway in the back of the hospital; An empty looking section of the facility. There were no other workers in this part of the hospital that I saw. The lights looked dimmer here than where I had been sitting the last 4 hours, and I was slowly developing a bad feeling the more we walked. The final hallway was a narrow one, with doors on each side, facing each other. This was reminiscent of solitary confinement sections of jails frequently shown on television. I was directed to enter the room at the end of the hallway and sit for a while and wait. Nobody told me what for. I thought my parents were coming to get me. There was a clear lack of communication here. I found out long after that this was a holding area for those who are a harm to themselves or others, brought on by mental illness. There were no windows in this entire block of the hospital, only doors. I sat in "my" room, waiting around for the next step to whatever is going on. The walls were bland and white, the floors looked like they belonged in a prison, there was one chair in the middle of the room, looking out in the direction of the room directly across from mine. When I first arrived in this unit, there was only one other person sitting in a room adjacent to mine, who struggled the same as me. There were no words said for hours. My room was right next to the entrance area the employees went in and out of. I remembered actually hearing a worker talk about me to her coworkers. Her words were "Yeah, so he apparently is really obsessed with his girlfriend and ended up making threats cause she rejected him or something like that". I knew she was describing my situation, but it wasn't accurate, and felt like a personal insult to me that she would speak of these things so close to my door. I believe this was one of the flaws of the system In place there for mental health patients. It didn't sound like a medical discussion, rather a gossip session between friends.

Hours and hours and hours passed. I would get out of the chair, pace the corners of this tiny white windowless room, sit back down in the chair, stare at the ceiling, rinse and repeat. The bathroom in this hallway was my only escape from the insanity, and I would be able to leave my room occasionally to walk across the floor into the bathroom reminiscent of a prison. This hallway was desolate, void of life. The employees rarely ever walked out of their own door, besides to walk right past us to go to a different area in the hospital. There was no clock in this place. The only sign of what time it was I ever had was from me asking a passerby nurse what time it is. I had spent the entire night in this unit with absolutely nothing to do, nothing to see, no one to talk to. I was faced with the realization that nobody is coming to save me. I am in here for the long haul. This nurse who informed me with the time was then asked by me "I am completely complying here. I have been since I was in police custody. Ask the Emergency room. I am not a threat anymore. Can't someone call my parents and get me out of here? No? Even with their suggestion? Is this legal?". She grew more annoyed with each question and told me I had to wait until a bed cleared up for me, but what exactly did she mean by "a bed"? I am already in a room by myself and just came from a bed in the ER. Her explanations came off as very vague to me, and weren't explaining what will happen to me. I still believed I may go to prison. There was no real input on what I could expect.

As morning approached every worker clocked out and a new rotation of people clocked in for their shift. Security personnel walked by at one point that afternoon and gave me an old mobile phone from the 90's to use for a quick call. I stupidly chose to call my girlfriend instead of my parents, and since it was the hospital's number and not mine, she picked up with a cheerful voice. "Hello?". I could hear loud music and other people in the background of this call. I literally couldn't believe what I was hearing. Not only did she, my partner of a year up until that point, have the police come to my house and take me away, while my parents cried their eyes out at home, and my siblings canceled personal trips to grieve the situation I was in, But here my girlfriend was, with the happiest toneI had ever heard her use, assuming I was someone offering her a job, seemingly having no signs of being upset or anything close to that. She, at the time of the call I later found out, was attending a festival with friends having the time of her life, while I was locked up in a cage with deep purple lines around both wrists from the cold and brutal handcuffs, as if I never existed to her. As soon as she heard my voice asking where she was, her tone dropped immediately, and responded with "Uhh? I can't.", That was it. Two words. No questions from her, not a single word about anything from her. She hung up the phone before I could say anything else. This was the very worst and most heartbreaking moment I had experienced in my adult life so far.

My stomach got worse, as the smell of food being brought to me once again was enough to convince me I needed to vomit. I hadn't eaten since Tuesday morning, and here we were at what had to be Wednesday afternoon and I still had no intention to eat. I knew I wouldn't keep anything down. I felt sick to my stomach both metaphorically and literally. The food tray stayed by my door that entire day. As several more hours passed, the number of patients filled the rooms in the hallway. It felt like I had been in there forever. There was no sense of any time passing once again. I grew uncomfortable with the chair and began pacing my room with my hands behind my back for several minutes at a time, then I would sit on the cold, hard floor and lean my back against the wall to relieve how crooked my back was becoming from so much time straining it while sitting with no back support all night and day. I would begin losing my mind. There was a time I looked at the blank wall, forcing myself to hallucinate so that I could pretend it was a window looking out to the free world. I grew increasingly frustrated and distraught, thinking loud but inside of my head "Oh Come on! It can't possibly take THIS long! They're *TRYING* to anger me so that i could start yelling at them and they can keep me in here even longer! What am I supposed to do?!". This was all inside of my head, since I knew very well that If I said anything that showed any bit of impatience or anger, after seeing my texts and knowing what I was in there for, they would surely make this experience much worse than it already was. I remembered the young police officer's words from the day before when he told me to let the process work itself out and that I need to just get through this and stay out of trouble because I got very lucky that no charges had been filed against me. I kept remembering that phrase and kept my cool, albeit still beginning to lose my mind. The constant pacing I had been doing started annoying the patient in the room directly facing mine, so I eventually stopped to avoid being looked at in that narrow cone of vision, as if it would have stopped him from glaring in my direction in the first place given how small of a sight of vision we had. I had a stroke of luck during my time here, as there were limited beds available in the floor upstairs, whatever was to come up there, hence the overwhelmingly long delay we all had to power through in the holding process. Why is this lucky for me? Well there was another patient in the room next to mine, and the staff had to choose based on various factors, which patients to export to a large mental hospital in another city an hour away. This would have been the end of me had it happened to me instead of the patient next to me. I narrowly avoided being sent up the highway to the equivalent of a prison sentence for the mentally ill. Had I been sent there, I was told I would have likely lived there for much more time and would have focused more on a vigorous rehabilitation type of approach rather than a routine mental health emergency type of commitment. During the final hours of this holding unit, my vision completely became caked over with blurriness. My face went motionless, not in a medical way, but due to me zoning out and completely shutting off. The constant staring at the wall, the hunger my body felt but my mind rejected, the dehydration from me refusing to touch the cup of water in fear that I would just hurl it up upon swallowing it, drained the glint in my eye and my mind began wandering off into its own separate world. I started ignoring my surroundings ultimately, which I am sure didn't make me look any more mentally stable to the staff.

The day came and went; One by one, patients had their time. We noticed a pattern inside this holding unit, where either a nurse, or a tech with a wheelchair would come and tell someone it is time to be transferred to their bed upstairs. Though I was one of the first patients inside of this hall, I was one of the last to go. Finally after an eternity, the staff member finally came to my door with that wheelchair. I questioned why this chair was needed, and I was told that it is a protocol in the hospital to be transferred this way from one part to another. I didn't dwell on this. I was just ecstatic to at last be moving on to the next step. When I asked for the time, I immediately was floored. After realizing it was now past 7:40. PM, All in all, I realized from the moment an employee escorted me from the ER into that section,I had spent a total of 23 hours in that holding room staring at that ugly, blank, empty, hopeless wall, on top of the 4 hours spent in the Emergency room waiting. My mental state evaporated so destructively in those 23 hours, I imagined how terrible it must be then for those in prisons around the nation who are thrown into solitary confinement and stuck there for months, some even years. This cannot be a healthy way to house anyone. My experience being in such a tiny, confined empty room by myself opened my eyes to the suffering of inmates who have a much worse time than I did, and was something that never really crossed my mind as I lived my civilian privileged life prior to my downfall. I was wheeled up a long corridor where there were more employees than I had seen up until that point. After riding in an elevator, I was rolled into a new area past a set of double doors. It looked much more colorful than the previous place I called home for just an hour short of a full 24 hours. Instead of prison-esque flooring and a solitary confinement feeling, It was replaced with now a carpeted floor, walls with photo frames on them and vastly more staff interaction with patients. I was hopeful that I would finally see this new doctor and be on my way, but as my luck went, my optimism came crashing down with yet another miserable blow right to the heart.

While being initially assessed, I was told by staff that since it was already night, the doctor I was scheduled to see was currently not there,and would be back in the morning. The words "Unfortunately, yes you will be staying here at least overnight, then we will figure out where to go from there, okay? Now let's show you around our amenities." brought me back to the same disappointment that I had in those holding rooms downstairs. Behind the friendly staff and warm facade of this area, I learned that it was the psych ward of this hospital. Unbeknownst to me, my emergency phase had ended, and my psychiatric stay began that wednesday night.

INVOLUNTARY PSYCHIATRIC STAY

I felt so helpless, with everything completely out of my control. For the first time in my life, my freedom and fate was completely up to another human, who has never met me before. This must be how first time criminal offenders must feel being booked into correctional facilities. Even though a psych ward within a hospital could not be compared to the horrors they deal with each day in prison, it still didn't make me feel any more free in my experience. After having my gruesome scars on my forearms examined, along with the leftover purple prints from the handcuffs, I was given my patient bracelet that I would have to wear until they were finished with me, reminding me that I had nowhere to run. I belonged to them for as long as they wanted me, and there wasn't a thing I could do about it. A nurse later took me on a tour of the psych unit in this hospital I would be calling home until I am released. I saw a television room, which looked no different from an informal waiting room. There was an art room, a couple consultation rooms where one would speak with a psychologist, a small cafeteria room with some tables for meals, then there were the patient's rooms, housing two in each of them. Though still not comfortable or uplifting in any way for me in the situation I landed myself into, this floor was spacious, and easier to manage space than the cramped dungeon I just came from. After taking this tour, Inside of my mind I panicked, because I was thinking to myself that this looks like it is meant to be a new home for me and they are planning on throwing away the keys and there was no sign in sight that I was ever going to leave. I had heard of cases on TV and in books where certain individuals in the world are deemed mentally unfit for society and are sent to live in psych wards and some of them never get out. They live their lives and pass away in there. Was this going to become my fate as well? I didn't bother asking that question, because I knew it would automatically be avoided by the staff and they weren't the ones who were going to be in charge of what happens to me. They were merely there to take care of me. Walking into the room assigned to me, I noticed it looked like a typical hospital patient room, minus the usual tile flooring. Safety was a key rule on this floor and I could tell, since most of us were considered to be a danger to ourselves. The floors were carpeted all throughout with the exception of the eating area, likely because almost every patient had their shoes taken from them. I can only remember a single patient who kept his shoes, but the laces were removed from them first. I believe he voluntarily admitted himself unlike me, being taken against my will. In my room, I reluctantly met my roommate, my elder by at least ten years. The sobering thought of what I could become in a decade if I did not try digging myself out of this mental imbalance struck me that night as there was nothing to do but really reflect on my life up to that point.We both kept to ourselves and had almost no interaction.

Patients here were encouraged to sleep, though how could I? The last day and a half for me had seen the world lifted from under me in such a short time and in an impactful fashion. That night, I mainly sat in a small room around the corner which contained coloring books and paper to draw on, but only with crayons, as they were not sharp as a pencil would be. This reminded me of an elementary school art room, which had its own smaller TV in case there was a certain program on in the television room and other patients wanted to watch something else. This room stood next to the actual art room, which housed several different activities besides painting. I only refer to this as the art room since it seemed to be the main theme of that section. Everything appeared to be organized in consideration for individuals who required distractions while being treated here. My mind was at the time still totally fixed on my girlfriend, unaware what she was up to, who she was with, if she had broken up with me. By then she was fully aware where I was and what was going on, but chose to separate herself from the situation. Every 15 minutes or so, employees would perform routine checks on each patient and occasionally check blood pressure, and make sure we took our prescribed medicines. I hadn't known this until then that I had been prescribed anxiety meds and had no choice other than to take them. I knew that if I showed even an ounce of resistance, I would likely be in trouble. My mind had been so tilted at this point, I believed any little slight sign of annoyance would result in the police coming back and throwing me in jail. I was also given a pill to help me sleep, as I knew I would be needing some kind of help if they expected me to get any rest at all. When the lights dimmed in the hallways, It was time to wind down. I cannot remember whether or not there was a designated bedtime, but I knew I chose when I went to bed. For the first night, after laying in my bed, the tears came for the first time since my arrest. Keep in mind from before, when I was a baby, it was said by older relatives that I rarely ever cried. Until this point, I never showed emotions of sadness like this. I turned to my side so that the other guy in the room didn't witness it, not that it mattered. He cried himself in that room previously in the night anyways. I still hated anyone being involved in my business, and to me, crying was a personal matter more than anything. This would prove to be the least of my worries as I would come to realize in the coming days.

It took seemingly an hour or so to fully fall asleep, if you can call it that. My eyes were closed for hours on end, but no true REM cycle until 4 hours into laying there. This was made difficult as staff would approach the door and peek inside to make sure no one was breaking any rules or harming anyone.The doors in these rooms never fully closed for this reason, so the dimmed lights from the hallway would seep into my room causing me to remain awake for longer than hoped for. I must have fallen asleep, because the next thing I remember is hearing a low volume announcement on the wall next to my bed. 8 AM was the morning announcement. An employee sounded off the morning activities and which time they were. These activities were "optional", but not optional. I was told I am not forced to go to group sessions, but if I chose not to, it wouldn't help me get out of there and that they would hold me for longer. It seemed disingenuous to me how they worded things here. I thought in my head "Well why don't you just tell me I'm forced to attend then? Quit with the B.S". I couldn't say this phrase because any sign of an attitude would be labeled as an aggression brought on by anti-social behavior. For the first day, I went along with the words that it was optional, so I opted out. I caught flack for this decision that morning by some of the techs who worked there. I also explained to them prior in paperwork that I did not eat in the morning because of a diet I was on, which was intermittent fasting. Staff still would come by and bother me and almost passively aggressively bully me into eating something. This wouldn't be a big issue at first, since they were more focused on getting me set up to see the physician in charge of my case. I had one nurse assigned to me, one doctor, and the rest were medical staff without higher titles such as those. The doctor entered my room and met me for the first time. She had vast knowledge on psychology and human behavior from what I can only imagine is countless years of education and practice. I cannot take anything away from her academic success and intelligence, but I believe we got off on the wrong foot almost immediately. Our understanding of my personal turmoil stood on totally opposite terms, and I say this with as much respect and well regard as I can, but she didn't convey much understanding nor empathy for me, at least from my perspective this is the case. Upon entering an interview room with her, I explained what led up to me being there and why I thought I was innocent. Yes, I actually attempted protesting for my freedom, despite the terrifying texts I had sent to others. This plea to be released only furthered her to use her professional expertise and see the obvious signs that I was growing highly delusional. While she was misunderstanding my explanation that I wasn't planning on harming anyone and that it was merely a scare tactic, I was ignoring the clear fact that I was unwell, and if i had gone home right then and there, I wouldn't have gathered any progress in my condition as needed. Anxiety attacks are uncontrollable from my own perspective, but in the medical sense, they could be prevented by numerous behavioral changes and tweaks to perception of stressful scenarios like the one I found myself diving into that month. I believed her theory on what is wrong with me to be true, but the solution to the issue she had given me was cliche, and sounded as if it came straight from a book. It didn't sit right with me. She seemed to suggest the solution to my anxiety was to find new outlets for my expression of sadness and stress besides cutting myself, which obviously is true. The part that didn't offer a solution was when she essentially attempted nudging me to give up on being with my girlfriend, not grounded from reasons of me scaring her to death and making threats, which would have sounded more of a reasonable excuse to tell me to break up, but rooted in the belief that if a couple argues, the underlying cause always comes from contempt for one another. Her reasoning was that she would only continue to be herself and on this basis, I would continue having panic attacks, and continue following the same destructive cycle over and over, bringing her down with me. I respectfully declined the idea of this. Her argument portrayed me as having a problem with my girlfriend as a person or something in her life, when in reality, she was only the unfortunate recipient of my bottled emotions being taken out, after months of low income frustration and our relationship suffering greatly from it, since she was the person I communicated with the most. I believed too that she knew this, and only stepped away from me to have a moment to work on herself and not just my crumbling life.

The first conversation with my assigned physician here was brief, and not the best I could have had. This however, wasn't designed to be my psych session. I would have that later in the afternoon with a licensed therapist working in the unit. He brought me into the art/activity room and mainly let me talk it out while he listened with a clipboard in hand jotting my words down. He stayed quiet most of the conversation, and gave his input where needed. His approach to the skillset of that job was interesting to say the least. I benefited from his method to make me perceive myself as more grounded than I was in reality. I would go on with my story and he asked about my hobbies. When I mentioned I watch TV to relax, instead of putting forth the usual spiel telling me what to do to make life easier and such, He responded with "Oh yeah! Have you ever seen that one TV show? Seems like everyone's watching that thing now. I don't get it. I think its kinda dumb but my kids watch it. I gotta sit through the lame jokes when I cook my breakfast. Makes me wanna go to work sooner." His response evoked my very first grin that whole week. I found his input on a television show he hated amusing, and could see myself saying something like that if I were in his place in life. He was relatable and used humor to break the ice a little. The placement of him in this ward was much needed. While others gave a grave serious vibe around the floor, he struck me as the type of guy who would tell me not to take life so seriously, then follow it up with a phrase taking humor from the dark aspects of life. Laughing at pain doesn't help for everyone, but this risk he took with my condition during the therapy session definitely worked for me. I didn't feel as though I was being scolded by a guy with a lot of diplomas on the wall, rather I felt like I was speaking with a friend or a neighbor about what had been going on, with the lighthearted jokes at how dark life can sometimes be sprinkled in to let me know he too was just a regular guy with his own set of problems and challenges, and he handles it differently than I do. I felt that I too could aspire to handle dark times with the same sarcastic energy as him. This was the design of his method, and it served as a remedy for my anger. I hadn't known this while he had this conversation with me initially, because I was still so pent up and in total shock from being basically locked up in a jail referred to as a hospital floor. I am sure he had a different approach for each patient he encountered, and tweaked his mannerisms accordingly, to make the conversations as comfortable as possible. He masterfully honed his craft and used it to make his work exceptional. I can say with confidence I believe he was meant to be in this job field. He sent me out to the hallway to continue my torturous indefinite stay at this miserable place.

The first treatment along with medicine was the new idea planted into my brain. So simple, yet incredibly hard to recognize from a short-tempered perspective, I pondered what it would have been like, had I simply responded to my girlfriend ignoring my texts as he might have. It would have been something similar to: "Ah She's using the silent treatment on me. Whatever, I won't be the bad guy when she needs me to kill a spider or reach the top of the fridge again", or something to that effect. Sarcasm and letting go, basically not giving a damn, can be a coping mechanism, and can be used as a way to get through uncomfortable moments in life for many. Using boxing as a metaphor, Instead of allowing the affliction of the haymaker to level me into the canvas, try rocking head movement along with the direction of the punch coming towards me, and the outcome will be an avoided knockout so to speak. If a fighter leans in towards the punch, it would surely hurt badly. Whether intentional or not on his part, that was a lesson I gathered from that particular psychologist.

I went back out into the hallways and began pacing aimlessly. I took laps around the entirety of that unit and would try looking out the double doors, knowing they were locked to keep all of us from ever getting out. I became aware of what each quirk had been for fellow patients here. Some were the introverted types like myself, while others had vibrant talkative energies about them. We all had our own separate reasons for being there, but it seemed becoming used to one another's varying personalities was one of the hardest parts of settling into our stay at first. There were a few clocks throughout the ward, and I at least had the ability to have a sense of the time being spent there. I soon realized that pacing laps in the same direction over and over 50 times over, turning a corner to only see a clock telling me that only 15 minutes had passed, I needed to find something to occupy me until the next person snatches me for a consultation. I finally convinced myself to enter the television room to try occupying my mind and getting the horrible thoughts of hopelessness to back off for a while, but I noticed that room had a few windows looking out. The unstoppable pain struck me as I glanced out into the free world, with everyone else I knew, and everyone my age living life without me. They were unrestricted, and here I was, reaping the consequences of my own mistake. A thousand scenarios went through my mind like a movie. I had thought of how I could be out there at work, going grocery shopping, driving my car; any little task I thought of as a drag out there seemed somehow exciting to me. Though miserable looking out, I did feel slightly hopeful, as I knew normality was not out of my reach. I had a choice to either be defiant the entire time in this facility, or to cooperate and hope the doctor notices I am trying and maybe lets me go home. I couldn't sit and watch the monotonous television sitcoms for too long, I needed to work on getting out of there. Idling in the recreation rooms wasn't going to help me in my mind. I still however turned down the various group sessions. I was told it wasn't "necessary", so I went on with my horribly depressing second day best I could. For lunch, I only ordered some crackers and some water. I merely ate to survive, as taking in any more than that would inevitably cause an upset stomach for me due to the anxiety of being in this stressful situation.

By the time evening came around, I refused dinner. I couldn't stand the smell of meats and vegetables other patients had ordered in that cafeteria, which was right across from my room. The nauseating scent of meatloaf, soups, and other sorts of full meals were too much for my stomach to handle. I was still dealing with the shock and trauma from the previous two days I had been locked in the hospital. I couldn't take down any food even if I tried to. I got tons of flack and intrusive scolding about this choice that night, which made my discomfort grow increasingly more restless. I simply wanted to figure out my options with a doctor, promise to never have an outburst again and be on my way, but this was clearly not on the agenda for this establishment. I still lived under the delusion that this would be a short ordeal. After being given stern words by staff on my eating habits, I retreated back to my dark room where I could have space to think. The window of my room overlooked the parking lot and some houses behind it. I tried limiting the amount of time spent leering at the outside world, but with the lack of options to keep me going in there, I felt this was my only activity that didn't involve unnecessary interaction with others. I heard a call from a nurse assigned to me telling me I had visitors. Who could it be? It was my parents! The same parents who feared for their lives and my life, who should have shunned me and kicked me out, yet they were here to see me in my time of need. The joy I felt, having their forgiveness was indescribable! I truly felt I had a second chance at life.

Since the final meal of the day had ended, the cafeteria was open for visitors to see patients. We congregated at an empty table to discuss what had happened, and before any of us could say anything, I looked them both in the eye and began crying my eyes out. The uncontrollable weeping went on for about a minute before I recapped everything that had gone down from the porch of our house, all the way to where I was at that point. I took solace in venting to my parents, rather than a licensed psychologist, as they knew the true me. They were the ones who brought me into this world, and witnessed my very first steps, my shortcomings, my achievements, my friendships, my hardships, everything. I trusted them above all else, to truly understand my intentions, and what went wrong in my head to bring me to such a scenario.

Once I finally figured out how to break the ice, we discussed everything for a good five to ten minutes before visiting time was up. We embraced and that was that. My parents were leaving for the day. I had to find something new to occupy myself with before I went insane in that place once they left. It was only a quarter past 8 PM at that point and I still had a big issue with being there in general. There was no chance I was going to be ready to sleep. I stupidly assumed my parents would give the staff some attitude and I would be set free, but evidently, I needed to accept that I was stuck in there for the long run. I waltzed into the smaller TV room where the patients in their twenties and thirties mostly congregated, while the middle aged and older ones mainly took the television in the larger room since we had different television tastes. I sat on the floor against the wall there, as five or six young adults filled up the seats and I did some observing. For the first time I felt semi-comfortable here, as if I was hanging out with likeminded people. We spent an hour or so watching late night comedy, which was perfectly appropriate for our age group that we could all laugh at. This was a nice memory for me, and I enjoyed actually laughing for once at the crude humor late night TV entails while I decompressed after a long day. We awkwardly would make small talk about anything and everything, ranging from our ages to our ethnicities. Was this what a normal conversation felt like? It was so alien to me that I was shocked that anyone would actually hit it off with me in a conversation, given my past experience with others. As the clock continued to move, I knew I needed a plan to be able to sleep again.

I didn't want to lay in that bed for hours staring at a ceiling so I walked down that short carpeted hallway to the staff's main desk and requested help with sleeping, and to my surprise my request was easily obliged without fuss. I had predicted that everyone was out to get me and anything I go through there was punishment, but the friendliness of some workers made me feel as though I was not being judged for my actions, but instead being treated as I very well was: a patient with mental illness. I was given a pill intended to make me drowsy to aid my sleep and I retreated back to my room where I spent my second miserable night in that cold bed. The psych unit in this hospital had a policy where a blanket couldn't surpass a certain meticulous measurement of thickness, to prevent patient suicides, so there was only a paper thin blanket available in my bed that only wrapped around my legs and nothing else, leaving me cold and irritated at night. My pillow had no pillowcase, and the lights from outside my room leaked in due to the doors being cracked open per hospital policy, so I believe the sleeping pills were definitely needed for me at the time. After forcing myself to drift to sleep, the next day approached. The speaker next to my bed went off notifying the unit of the 8 AM and 11 AM activities for the morning and I dreaded the inevitable nagging from someone telling me to attend, and sure enough a nurse had told me that if i went to the group sessions, it would help me in the long run because it would show to the doctor that I was really trying and improving, so I ultimately decided to walk down the hall to check it out and see what I could do.

The therapy room had chairs arranged in a circle like in a typical setting you'd see in the movies, so that detail was already inducing anxiety, knowing that I always have been downright terrible at conversation, especially emotional ones with deep stories. I wanted to back out but the door was already closed by the time I sat down, so I remained in my seat while the therapist came in. Luckily for me, the one leading this session was the funny down to earth therapist from before. Seeing him made me feel a little more comfortable staying there, since we already talked before about things and he was able to observe my quiet demeanor. The room was packed, with nearly every patient in the ward attending, minus a few holdouts. The therapist went around the room clockwise and each of us had to say our names, and why we were there, and what we would like to accomplish there. For the first time, I was publicly candid about my hideous scars on my arms. I showed the 15+ other patients each arm and what was basically "wrong" with me. At first it was embarrassing, but honestly, I knew everyone would understand me. I was not the only one who had a history of cutting in the psych ward, but my scars were the most recent, and the deepest ones. All up and down my right arm were nine dark gashes, along with one long diagonal cut down my left arm. They were so noticeable, that if you met me for the first time, the scars would be what you saw first, not my facial features or anything else for that matter. The scars stood out aggressively compared to the others. I am unsure if I was the youngest patient here, but I was definitely among the youngest. The scars seemed to shock the older patients in their 50's and 60's more than anyone, as I came off originally as mild mannered and quiet to them, they wouldn't imagine I would be so violent and emotionally destructive to my body. Most people that I had known in my life up to that point could never imagine such a thing either, but with anyone in the world, I had my dark secrets. The group tell-all felt arbitrary and nonsensical at the time, but upon reflection, I think part of the reason they bunched us all in a tight space like that was to give us the visual proof that we really aren't that crazy as people say we are, and that there are so many more individuals out there who handle social capabilities and mental coping mechanisms a little differently than the conventional system in place in society. It was oddly comforting for me spilling my guts to total strangers, since seeing an emotional wreck with scars wasn't out of the question in their world, but in the "normal" world it had been seen as terrifying. Though they had just met me, these patients knew what I was going through.

The time was moving so slowly. I finished a morning session and I still had no idea whatsoever what exactly was going to happen with me, or if I was ever going home. I exited the therapy room and was immediately approached by the doctor who visited me the previous day. Suddenly, relief washed over me and I instantly became overly optimistic. I was finally going home? She brought me into a room and discussed my condition further. I continued to basically beg to be sent home, and even told the doctor to call my parents and that they would tell her that I was not an actual risk and to send me home. Little did I know that they did actually request my release the night before and it was declined by the doctor, who felt I needed further evaluation. She explained that there is no way of really knowing what I would and wouldn't actually act on, especially seeing that my arms proved that I had been a man of action when it comes to taking out frustrations on myself, why should she believe I wouldn't act on my threats towards others after all? I completely understood her reasoning, but my denial and panic took over and I kept politely arguing my innocence and a need to go home. The doctor prescribed me anxiety medication and concluded the chat. I was once again left to wander the ward trying to figure out what is going to happen. I went into my room to drink some water and maybe take a nap, when I was approached by an employee letting me know that I had a call for me. I excitedly got up and rushed to the phone. I expected my parents to call and check on me, but as soon as I put the ear to my phone, my hospitalization became dark. My girlfriend's voice came through, and my heart completely dropped. Immediately we both rushed to apologize, even though this was really my own doing. I told her that everything was okay and I am waiting to get out of that hospital, and asked if she would wait for me so we could talk it out. In the middle of my sentence, she eagerly hurried to say "I'm sorry. I just can't. I'm sorry. I really think I can't see you any longer. I'm sorry." I responded with "Wait, please. I will change. I went through hell. Please don't leave. Can we at least talk about this, please? Please..." She finished with "I'm sorry. I have to go. Maybe in the future when everything is different but not now. We can't be together. I'm sorry. Bye." and before I could let out my first word she hung up. I looked back at the employee, and she had a look on her face as if to say "I know what just happened. I'm sorry". I gave the phone back and took a brisk walk back to my room, where I slipped into the bathroom and looked in the mirror. I let a stream of tears flow down my face like I never before, even more tears than that talk with my parents, because not only had I lost my family, but now my partner was gone forever. The hopelessness and pure anguish washed over me and the tone of my stay in the psych ward changed. I was stuck there, and my girlfriend was running off with another guy, my siblings would never see me ever again, and all I have left is my parents. In that bathroom I started thinking to myself: What comes when I get out of here? No one will ever look at me the same. Forget about getting a job now, and my chances of ever coming around my girlfriend or her family after this? Not a chance. I'll never celebrate a holiday or birthday ever again, and my reputation and image is forever tarnished. Even if I somehow get back to society, I will have to relocate. There is no way I will be able to even do grocery shopping in this small town with my girlfriend living there with another man, and all of my family and their friends who know what happened to me by now. I cannot show my face anywhere!

When dinner time came around, I knew I had to eat something or I would have a serious physical complication, so I requested that I eat in my room because I never liked sitting in a room full of a million people while they stare at me eating. This is not a problem for me, and I have lived with this quirk my entire life. This was not a factor to me being in that hospital. My frightening behavior was. That being said, after being scolded by staff about me somehow ruining their day because I preferred to eat in peace, they obliged, and I ate a small salad with some water and crackers at the desk in my room. If they wanted me to eat, I was going to do it my way. Some would see this as me being stubborn and snobby, but I am a simple introverted person. I want my peace and quiet. That doesn't make me a psychopath, though for some reason this seemed to give off red flags for the hospital. I was already going through a breakup and trying to eat through my nausea, and the constant checking on me and suggestions from the workers was beginning to pile up and create a headache.

Once I finished my meal and took another prescribed sleeping pill, I put my head in the pillow on my bed and immediately went to sleep. At this point I was in a deep trench in my own mind. The next morning came, and I was still in disbelief at what happened the past few days. My beard started growing, I started noticing my face getting thinner from the lack of calories, and I hit an all time low just within a couple of days. I was hoping that I would wake up and find out the whole thing was just a bad dream. I had nothing to lose at that point, so I continued to attend morning meetings to make myself look better to the doctor. I noticed a pattern, that she would come around each morning after the 8 AM therapy activities, so I expected to see her again and plead to be released. I had another discussion with her as usual, and I grew visibly and verbally frustrated. She told me "You have been attending the sessions and we see this. We are going to wait a few days until the medication works itself into your system first to see how it goes. For now we see you have heightened social anxiety still so we are going to observe that still." I was told that since it was friday, and the mental facility does not release patients on weekends, I was required to stay there for at least the entire weekend regardless. She stated "social anxiety" was the main reason I was being held. I couldn't believe that I was completely at the mercy of this one lady who knew nothing about me or my life, all over one private text message to someone who is not her, that she did not know the actual context of. I explained to her initially that I was only using a scare tactic in the form of threats in my first real relationship that I didn't know how to handle, but she wasn't buying it. My case looked too similar to others who end up in prisons. She was in complete control of me. Not that it was her fault. She was only doing her job. These are the types of cases that come through those doors every single day. In the grand scheme of things, I was merely paperwork with a common situation.I feel like most mental health emergencies are treated too similar, and every scenario is placed under an umbrella. I will later explain why I feel this is wrong. After she was on her way, I chased her down the hall politely and approached her. "Look, I know why I am in here. It is because of my arms and my threats I have said to others, but You shouldn't be able to keep me in here just because of what you call social anxiety. That's not my fault. I have no problem with my personality. It's everyone else! Me deciding to eat in my room was simply because I am an introvert, not some spooky problem with my brain that makes me crazy. That has nothing to do with any of this", and the doctor took this as me challenging her to an argument, because she later called my parents and told them I was being rude and confrontational.

How could I cope with the news that I will be trapped indefinitely, on top of the fresh heartbreak? I had absolutely no other choice besides trying to make the most of the time I was forced to stay there. I attended the 11 AM activity of the day, which was a word association quiz of sorts. Honestly, I don't remember exactly what the nature of this word game was, but I do remember that this session took place in the large art room. I noticed a couple of different board games, a long table, a couple of highly monitored music instruments, and large windows looking out towards the plaza across the street. I'll never forget daydreaming out that window watching the world go by without me. I noticed people across the street at a plaza buying coffee. I noticed I was also undergoing a caffeine withdrawal, since they did not allow any coffee in the ward. This area became more of a hangout than an activity room. Nothing noteworthy went on here, but I was just trying my very best to kill as much time as I could. My stomach had been growling since Tuesday, but I knew I couldn't eat a bite, and a few days into the commitment, the staff began imploring me to eat something, anything. My refusal to take in any nutrition and barely some water, was doing just as much harm to my health as my mental state was. My nurse informed me that this was another larger reason why I wasn't released yet. When the afternoon snack came around, I finally ate my second meal, a tuna salad sandwich and a small cup of green beans. It was all I was willing to consume for the time being. The nervous feeling in my stomach kept me uneasy most of the time while locked in the facility, since I was constantly thinking my then ex girlfriend was already out with another man rebounding. I remember almost nothing about the weekend, other than purposefully waking up late and I kept having to constantly tell the staff every single morning that I do not eat breakfast and It was not anything to do with my mental health, but a diet I had been on. Nothing more. I had brief discussions with the nurses and other staff during the weekend through the days, asking as many questions as I could pertaining to me going home. They continuously would explain to me that I wasn't going home until the doctor decided I was fit to leave. I knew they weren't kidding either, as I witnessed one patient being told he was required to have a longer 90 day stay at one point. I had to play along with the game, or I would be swallowed up by it. I knew that I had to learn what I can from this experience and never return, but also work on myself as a human being and understand how my outbursts and turmoil effects others around me. However, i learned right then and there, that getting released from an involuntary mental hospitalization is tricky, and definitely requires the right performance. I believe they were a bit too strict with some, and relied on going by the book, rather than using a human to human approach.

In a psych ward, EVERY single action you take, small and big, is constantly under a microscope 24/7.

- Facial expressions
- Tone of voice
- Way you walk and carry yourself
- Speech frequency
- Frequency of showering and brushing teeth
- Mood
- Meal frequency
- How long you sleep

These were all determining factors to staff reporting on my progress. If you walk around with a grumpy facial expression, or wear the same outfit all week, or shower only once a week, or lay in bed all day and not attending any therapy sessions, you are under much more scrutiny than someone who follows orders without question, at least this seemed to be the case for me. I was nudged a few times by technicians in the ward that I could be held there more days, if I wasn't eating enough, or appeared to be neglecting any areas of hygiene or nutritional needs. I swiftly followed this advice, and began turning around my gloomy personality over the weekend in an attempt to look less of a risk to the outside world. I learned that the doctor in charge of my case did not work on weekends, and that I would see her on monday, so I did all i could to impress the staff available to me, to show them that I was not a threat to society, but instead just a broken man who has harmed myself and never wants to be in this situation again. I walked the halls of the unit saying hi to everyone and striking up small conversations with other patients in the television room, basically pretending to be someone I was not. They wanted a happy-go-lucky extrovert in my mind, so I was giving them one. I ate regular meals, even breakfast just to please them, even though it was strictly against my diet to eat that way. I began using the shower in my room, which was extremely uncomfortable to me, due to the fact that all doors in each room must remain slightly opened at all times, so the staff can perform their routine 15 minute checkups. I requested a shave, which was surprisingly pleasant. At home, I hated shaving and it seemed like such a drag, but here in this psych unit, It was a change of pace for me. They took me into a room I hadn't had access to before Sunday, and under supervision at the door, I shaved. I felt clean, well fed, and like a new man. My parents stopped by for a minute to bring me a fresh wardrobe to get through the rest of the time. I never felt so motivated to work on myself. It was out of fear and forcefulness of me being basically jailed in a hospital, but I would be lying if I said it didn't feel nice to take care of myself. I was taking my best shot at cleaning my mood up. My eyebrows generally always looked angry my entire life from genetics, but to the unaware workers watching me, I looked like I was angry at everyone. I uncomfortably muscled my eyebrows up and walked around with an expression of happiness the whole weekend, even though I was absolutely dying inside in every way. I was so frustrated that I felt I had to do these things to go home, but what I had been doing the past week was not helping me in the slightest. I had to do the complete opposite of laying around begging for help. I needed to conform. Since I was in this robotic state going through the motions, I remained in a fog for the rest of the weekend.

Monday morning, I woke up early anticipating my doctor's visit. It was finally a weekday again. They just had to send me home now right? I had been held here since last Tuesday night against my will with no clear release date. It surely has to be coming. When she greeted me for another consultation, my improvement was noticed. I did mentally evolve since my arrest, and knew from the moment I was handcuffed the week prior, that I was never going to get myself in this situation ever again. The part of me that was fake was the pleasant and cheerful attitude I exhibited to her. This meeting went better than the previous ones, as I didn't ask anything about going home. She acknowledged this and mentioned the weekend staff's notes about me beginning to congregate with others and eat meals, along with showering more often and acting less closed in. She however still never gave me a release date. I felt betrayed by the whole system they had set up there, but I couldn't argue with her, because I had reason to believe she would see that as me being mentally unhinged again, so I kept quiet and went on with my day. I attended the morning session as usual, and this time it was a social worker doing the assessment. She asked us what questions or concerns we may have and what we are doing to try working on our various mental illnesses. I raised my hand and brought up the concern that nobody has any information or timelines on when anyone is supposed to be leaving the facility, or if we are just stuck there forever. While we were being cared for and treated with medicine there, It was not ideal as a permanent solution either way. The friendships I developed with a few of the other patients here paid dividends, since we all had the opportunity to discuss these things together while watching television the day prior. One patient added to what I said and agreed with my concern, as they've been locked in there since Tuesday night along with me in the holding area from the lower floor. We had both been in it for the long run, and saw new people come and go before we ever had any information ourselves on what would happen to us. The social worker assured us that she would check these things in the computer and discuss the longer than usual hospitalizations with our doctors. I remember while being in the holding unit, I remember being unnecessarily stuck down there for so many more hours than the hospital allowed, because there were no beds available for patients upstairs, because those in charge of their stays were not letting any of them go home. Now I was in this same spot, and I knew I was taking up someone else's bed, and therefore, their time and progress. This was frustrating on a very personal level, knowing that someone is spending 23 hours down there just like me, because they would not release me and let me be on my way.

After the meeting concluded I was once again left in the dark and had to make the most of my time. My breakfast and afternoon snack went by as usual, and by the time evening came, I knew that if I was going home, it wasn't going to be today. The disappointment bothered me, but I can't say I was surprised. There was a clear lack of communication between medical professionals and the patients, not regarding needs of treatment, but on an information basis. I had no choice but to assume that I was expected to literally live there until I was shown mercy. I haven't breathed fresh outside air or worn shoes for an entire week at that point. My girlfriend disappeared into the past, and I haven't had any privacy either. The purple lines around my wrists from the handcuffs were still there, and that nagging medical bracelet required to wear on my wrist felt like a replacement for the handcuffs. It served as a constant reminder that I wasn't going anywhere. Dinner that night was my favorite, mostly because I actually bothered to try enjoying myself a little. Why not? I had nothing better to do and I was trapped regardless so I ordered a larger dinner than previous nights, which was a chicken sandwich, carrots and chocolate milk. It was enough to keep me satisfied through the night and I even had a small container of hospital ice cream after for extra calories.

After getting bored of some post-dinner television, I paced in laps around the tight hallways that surrounded the activity rooms and nurse's desk, ending up back on the hall where the rooms were. I was given the privilege of using a pencil, regardless of my known past of harming my arms, since I displayed a calm and focused mental state the past week and had asked for something to do. I drew a large tree on a piece of paper back in my room, with eyes coming out of each branch, as if they were lights installed onto leaves. The tree rooted out of rocky soil next to a river. This drawing was all I could think of for now, so I added as much detail to what I made in that picture. It acted as a symbol for me to this day, to remember that just as I rooted from nothing, I grew into a tree of branches that are my life paths, and I went down a wrong branch, which resulted in constant surveillance and eyes on me all day every day. My reckless actions caused me to spiral into personal chaos, resulting in so many strangers asking me personal questions and invading my personal space daily. I handled my own emotions and mental health incorrectly, and a spur of consequences followed.

While laying in bed around 11 PM that night, I couldn't sleep, because right outside of my door was the small cafeteria where we ate our meals. Four or five patients were sitting around the table and laughing about something and enjoying themselves. I didn't want to say anything because I was the last person who wanted to be a buzzkill. These individuals were going through a living hell just like me, so who was I to try taking away the only fun and smiles they probably would have there? I kept quiet, though both me and my roommate were visibly tired and a bit irritated from the noise. I buried my head into the pillow to sleep and eventually I settled down.

Tuesday morning came, and it was officially the one week mark for me in this hospital. I was so tired mentally and physically, but remained focused on my task to take care of myself, be polite to others, realize where I went wrong and move on. The first morning meeting went off without issue, and we discussed stories from our childhoods and old memories in life that stick with us.

For breakfast after I had some cereal and toast and got up for my routine laps around the unit when I approached the social worker lady once again. She let me know that she was in talks with my doctor and that I was likely getting released wednesday or thursday!! Finally! I was getting close to actually becoming free once again to start all over and become a better version of myself! My doctor briefly saw me, and discussed that if I would be released that week, that I would promise to not see things so black and white anymore, and to approach relationship or family problems with calm and patience. I was informed of many other ideas of how to release bottled stress besides cutting and yelling. Buying a punching bag was suggested, taking jogs, learning a new sport, and doing art were among the methods suggested to me. I took heed, because I knew that her word was the authority in that situation. She concluded our talk and my process continued. The last thing I remember doing was sipping some water and looking out the window of my room and the social worker approached me again, this time for the final time. She said "Okay we have you set up for a release today at 4:30 PM. Would you be okay with this time?"

I have never been so relieved since my birth. My entire face and shoulders completely relaxed into place and I said thank you about ten times before she went on her way. I was finally ready, after seven full days to leave! I ate my final afternoon snack and enjoyed it. I ate a little extra knowing that I was going to be unshackled within a couple of hours and took my laps around the halls for the last time. I felt bad knowing that I was leaving and others in this ward were stuck here for weeks, some would go on to stay there for months I am sure. I hadn't realized until that point that I built some necessary friendships with other patients and even some of the staff while I stayed there in that ward, and I regretted leaving some of them behind, specifically my roommate, who was an elderly man. He was grumpy just like me, but grew to enjoy my company and we appreciated each others' willingness to establish privacy and respectful barriers in our room we had to share. Unfortunate and tragic events led to fate cramming us together in a miserable and dark little room in a mental facility, but we fought the good fight together and suffered as like minded men from different generations. There is a strength in suffering together with someone else in that way.

I packed my clothing up in a bag and sat at my room's window looking out, anticipating my parents' arrival at 4:30. The final hours dragged on since I was so anxious to get as far away from that hospital as possible. When they showed up, they had my cell phone, wallet and keys in a brown paper bag, and my shoes ready for me at the elevator. I first had to sit down with a therapist and confirm that I was ready to go, and if I had any reason to believe I would be a risk to myself or others. I gave her an emphatic no and signed my final paperwork to exit there. My official diagnosis upon exit was: Major Depressive Disorder, and Severe Anxiety. I was prescribed medicine for this permanently and sent on my way after a full week of hell. I met my parents and put my shoes on. I noticed it felt so strange to actually wear shoes. We take for granted how comfortable we are sometimes wearing shoes. I had been hurting my heels the whole week on that hard carpeted floor that I was shocked at the relief I felt putting on some sneakers. My parents walked me out and I was already showing signs of a mental issue even larger than the one I entered the hospital with.

WHAT THE MEDICAL FIELD GETS WRONG

I stepped outside into a brand new perspective on life, breathing in the outdoors for the very first time in a whole week. It was so exhilarating! I was incredibly happy and energized to be back to the outside world, but something still felt very wrong. A new type of paranoia owned me. I felt that I had to walk on eggshells for the rest of my life in all aspects. I had an argument with my parents in the car because of a required appointment that was scheduled for me upon exit by the doctor and my parents told me that if I didn't attend that appointment, they would probably come grab me and take me right back into that psych ward. The argument only lasted a couple of seconds, and my parents told me something along the lines of: "See? You're arguing with us. You're gonna go right back to the hospital like that" and I realized that now everyone mentally felt like they had authority over me since I was the one who had been in trouble. I narrowly avoided being charged with a crime and was lucky enough to get off with that short hospital stint, so i honestly had no room to complain about the way the medical community had put restrictions on my life, but I felt offended that my parents gave me the impression that if I show any emotion, any opinion or any words that countered anything they said, I was going to burst out in rage and start screaming at people and that disagreeing with people equated to psychotic rage.

I had stayed overnight for seven days which had given me an opportunity to really observe the medical process and how mental patients are regarded in hospitals. This is in no way a hit piece of any sort. I have the utmost respect for the numerous staff members on the psych floor where I was held, especially the doctor who had to put up with my complaining the most, but I would have deep regrets if I do not voice my concerns with some areas of treatment of patients in mental emergencies and involuntary commitments in hospitals.

The first issue I notice is the way I was spoken to. I am a grown adult, and some of the staff used a tone of voice as if I was a toddler who had spilled apple juice on the floor. It felt very patronizing and I can't be the only one who felt that way. When I arrived there I felt like the employees saw themselves as somehow "above" us patients, because they were in a better place mentally than us. That's just how I felt. Not once have I been approached by a worker there as an adult, besides my initial meeting with the first therapist who was ironic and humorous. Other than him, the conversations with the nurses and other staff felt like I was a child asking an adult for help at times.

Another big problem that I feel should be addressed, is the lack of accommodation for different cultures and lifestyles in the psych ward. Examples I brought up earlier were my eating habits, and how I just wanted to be left alone. Since I was merely a baby, I kept to myself and conversed with my small circle. I never needed anything more than this. Most of the staff had been constantly approaching me and attempting to make me change a certain way I socialize, and tried dictating when and how I eat, and I felt as though my reserved and closed in personality was being used by the system in place as an excuse to keep me against my will for so many more additional days than actually necessary. I was involuntarily committed for self harm and being a threat to others as a result of anxiety attacks, but NEVER for being too shy or antisocial, though they saw these behaviors as an issue. I am a straightforward person for the most part. I shouldn't have been required to put on a fake personality to impress anyone in that unit. I might have a grumpy look on my face naturally, and maybe

I don't use eye contact as much as I should, and I come off as contentious with some people, but that shouldn't be anyone else's problem but my own, and my personality shortfalls should not have had an impact on my stay in the hospital.

Being in limbo in the emergency room also was not very helpful. I initially went through a full on mental health emergency and needed to be treated as such, yet I was placed on a bed and told to wait there for almost five full hours before being sent to the holding unit, which was even worse. The truth is, people such as me who have known heightened anxiety and different social capabilities than others, mostly want the process to be as smooth as fast as anyone else would want theirs to be. I saw no reason why I had to be held in the holding room for 23 full hours. That time I spent there was a step too far. For an emergency admission, I was not being handled as such on the first night and day of my hospitalization.

But the largest part that the medical professionals tend to get wrong the most about mental health patients, are the patients themselves. I fully understand that doctors and nurses may have a generally good education on the effects on behavior and brain when it comes to mental health, but facts are facts. If a person has not gone through mental disorders themselves, they can not fully know exactly what they are explaining when it comes to certain topics regarding a mental health emergency. This would also include some highly educated professionals. There is an explanation for this. Physicians can objectively see and diagnose physical health conditions because they are able to visibly see one's whole body, and with x-ray technology, this has become easier than ever. This also includes the brain and while there is a generally strong relationship between brain and an individual's personality, an unusually deep depression and random feelings of complete dread that plague those with mental illness on a daily basis, these things cannot be objectively observed other than the actual perspective of the one experiencing it themselves, since it is not an outwardly visible ailment, unless a brain tumor or other cognitive abnormality surfaces on the visual level to accompany it. Many mental illness sufferers are misunderstood in this regard, and umbrellas begin being placed over a vast amount of symptoms someone with psychological stress may live with. Some illnesses are caused by a certain physical trauma to the head, while others may be caused by post traumatic stress disorder. Some cases arise from environmental and social factors. I am unsure which category mine would fall under, but I do know that I do not fully agree with my diagnosis I was given while being released.

I fully accept the severe anxiety diagnosis. I have always had this issue from childhood. I would go out of my way to avoid human contact so that I do not have to deal with a simple conversation that anyone else would have been okay with. I never nailed the art of conversation, and have been known to be incredibly socially awkward. I understand this, and still to this day my awkwardness persists. I don't see my social anxiety going away, or the PTSD that I have developed from my hospitalization, but the major depressive disorder is where things get confusing for me. I have never thought of myself as a "depressed" person. Yes I had dealt with hopeless depression during my unemployed period living with my parents. I was living through a very rough time and being very poor, crammed into a house with my parents, after knowing what it was like to be free. I lost a lot in my early twenties, and that created a temporary misery and depression, but I do not believe I developed a major depressive disorder that is a part of my psychology or daily life. The depression I experienced was purely situational and environmental in my case. While living on my own with my girlfriend in my own home with a nice job, I was the most stable I could be. Depression can act like a sprain in the brain, that should not be pressed further on much like a twisted ankle, or could be genetic in many cases. I believe my social issues and behavioral problems stem from a genetic disposition, but I personally do not believe I really experience depression in it's true form at least in a way that affects me in a real way that I know of.

Many things I had explained to me by the doctor assigned to me I felt was simply wrong, since I had just met her and she was attempting to tell me all about myself and what I personally needed and I was being scrutinized for personality traits of mine that have not caused any problems for me in life at all (My "angry" eyebrow expression and choice to eat by myself are good examples). The whole staff there got to check out and go home after their shift ended, and I would watch out the window as they got into their cars and went off to their lives, while me and everyone else had to sleep there. Nobody could come and rescue us. We couldn't just go home like employees did. It seemed disingenuous at times hearing a few workers make it seem like they personally cared about our struggle, then clocked out of work like we never existed. The care I received was more transactional and routine, than understanding and compassion. I tried keeping myself together the best I could without arguing with the medical professionals I came across during my involuntary commitment. There were times where I felt like flatout telling them "Look, you don't know me or why I am here. You don't know what I go through and you don't know how to tell me what to do because you do not have my problems", but I knew that this would have been counterintuitive and unhelpful. I knew that the doctor knew best about medicine and she has dealt with thousands of other patients just like me, so I technically couldn't tell her that she didn't know what she was talking about, but I did not have the social skills to try explaining to her that every case is vastly different and we all should not be handled the same way because each one of us requires separate and varied approaches for treatment. This is a large conundrum for those who suffer with a mental illness, because many feel as though they do not have the right to speak up and suggest nuance in their own treatment of it. There are very few voices out there who are encouraged enough to feel that they know themselves more than a doctor would. I truly believe there are many with psychological illnesses who are afraid to speak up that they are receiving wrong treatment, due to the large stigma surrounding mental health that seems to insinuate that psychological disorders somehow disqualifies an individual from having the right to be correct or know anything about themselves. In a way this creates a barrier.

STIGMA & CONCLUSION

My time spent in a psych ward changed my life in many ways. I have a great deal of trouble with summer time, as my arms have never fully healed from the deep cutting. I wear longer sleeves most of the time to hide my shameful past from others. This is less about embarrassment, and more about me not wanting to scare people. The media and general discussion in society has created a false image about the millions of PTSD sufferers out there, that they are violent, or that if someone has been mentally hospitalized or is on medication for anxiety, that they would end up killing others. I was once told by an acquaintance "hey you look like the type of guy that'll end up shooting up a mall someday". I took a lot of offense to this for obvious reasons. I am an upstanding citizen just like everyone else. It hurts that the way I look down while talking to others or choosing to be introverted scares people so much that they would make horrible assumptions of my character and moral compass. It bothers me and I'm sure many others, that the negative stereotypes about mental health patients have dominated the news and have been pushed out as if it were gospel truth. It was never morally damning to have been diagnosed with psychological health conditions. More humans on earth have conditions than most would think, whether it be slight obsessive compulsive disorder, all the way to schizophrenia. The range is wide on this topic. It actually seems common these days. Some people are just a little different from the popular status quo, and march to the beat of their own drum. I fall under this category.

Finding new friends is tricky now that the past couple of years of my life has unfortunately led to me seeking them out much less, and dating is not much of a chance with my scars and all. The mere sight of them would scare anyone away.

Has the hospitalization helped me, or damaged me more? It is hard to say honestly. I do know one thing: Before entering that hospital, I had zero coping skills with anxiety, and expressed it through threats to others as a means to scare them into leaving me alone, and self harming to release the stress, but now since I was essentially scared straight, and given the proper treatment for these issues, I use my anxiety to be creative instead and find healthy outlets for expression. Everybody has a different outcome from police custody and emergency admission. When I first got home from the hospital, I developed paranoia that I believe became worse than the anxiety that led me to be there in the first place. I noticed a cop car on my street that day in front of a different house, and I became so engulfed in fear that I hid in my bathroom for thirty minutes or so, even though the police officer was not on the street for me and had nothing to do with me. My experience with the detainment and police van I went through resulted in some serious trauma afterwards, and often when I see a police car or that hospital in the distance in town, I instantly do feel a little anxious. It will likely always be a part of my life and is burned into my memory forever.

Another thing that changed significantly for me is what does and doesn't get a reaction out of me. I noticed ever since my release, that I no longer participate in road rage either. When someone tries creating a problem in a public place, I simply just walk away because I have no time for their games whatsoever at this point, and desire to live freely from drama, and all that comes with it. I know all too well that saying the wrong things leads to big trouble, and doing the wrong thing leads to even worse. I can say will complete confidence, that now at the age of 25, I have not cut myself at all since the age of 22 before my mental health emergency. My relationship with those in my circle remains great, and I look back at my traumatic seven days in a psych ward as an unwanted blessing and an important opportunity to become the best version of myself in this world and more importantly, to uphold a healthy mindset and worldview onwards, that I wouldn't have been able to realize had I not been taken into police custody that fateful day three years ago. My biggest takeaway of it all: To live the best I can and use a negative experience to create positivity out of it.

- Leo W. Monfore